Counting on Fall

written by
Lizann Flatt

illustrated by
Ashley Barron

Do you think that math matters to the animals and plants?

What if nature knew numbers like you?

Let's look at the fall.

Can you imagine what counting could do?

Who'd count the leaves
falling from trees,
stirred and disturbed
by the passing breeze?

As more
and more
fall to the forest floor,
the less there are left on the trees.

**Without counting, where
do you see more leaves?
Where do you see fewer leaves?**

And the less on the trees,
the more on the floor,
until the trees
stand there nakedly.

Guess how many leaves
are on the ground.
Count them if you'd like.

What number of nuts would the squirrels stash away?
Would they keep count? Would they keep score?
Imagine them comparing the size of their stores.

Can you count each
squirrel's acorns?

When fall fruits drop — plop, plop-plop-plop.
And seedpods pop — pop, pop-pop-pop.
Would they fall in neat patterns?
Would they float into rows?

Without counting, do you know how many fruits or seeds are in each group?

Do you think whales would race
to a sunny, warm place?

**Which whale is first? Which whale is last?
What places do the other whales hold?**

If honk-honking geese
kept to groups ten apiece,
what a sight that would make
at the lake.

Can you see several ways to make up ten?
Can you think of other ways to make ten?

Would pronghorns pair up,
line up in a parade,
and prance across the prairie?

Can you count the pronghorn
antelopes by twos?

With toes like those,
do you suppose
raccoons can count on trouble?

Can you count the toes by fives?

Might monarchs make sure
their roosts are arranged
so they're tucked up just so in ten rows?

**Can you count the
butterflies by tens?**

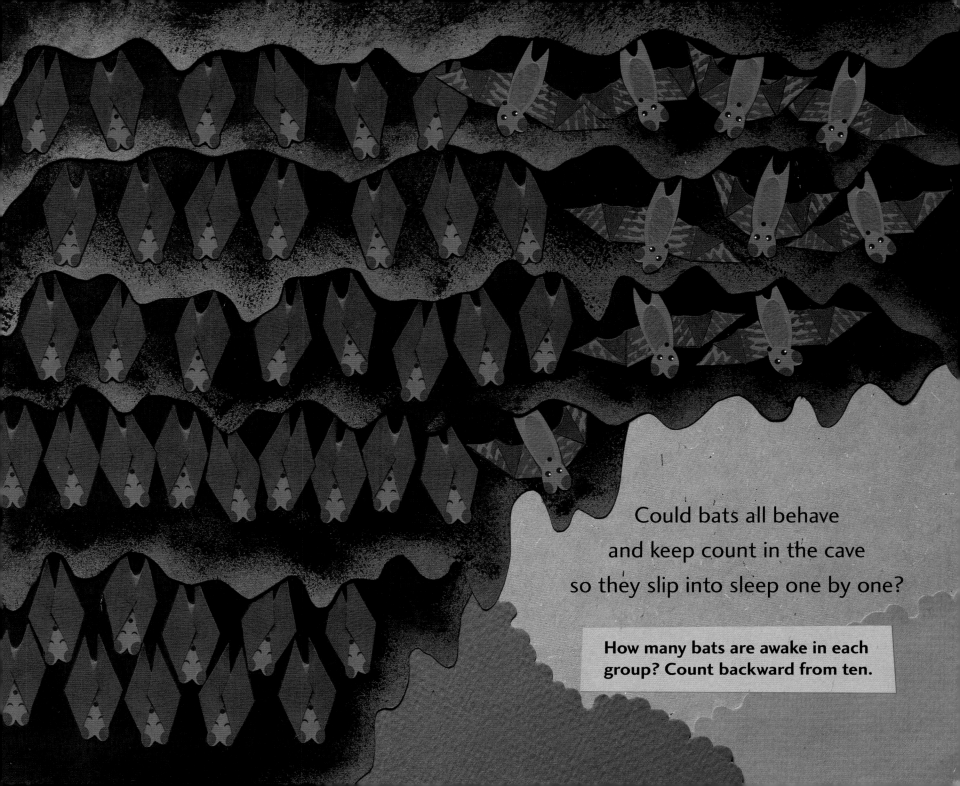

Could bats all behave
and keep count in the cave
so they slip into sleep one by one?

**How many bats are awake in each
group? Count backward from ten.**

When pikas pack away
piles of wildflower hay,
would they promise to pack the same number?

How many pikas are there?
How many piles does each pika have?
How many piles are there all together?

If the bears were aware,
would they think that it's fair,
if one were to gobble
more than his or her share?

Which bear has 2 berries more than 5?
Which bear has 2 berries less than 10?

A flock of cackling grackles awakes,
ready to leave the tree.
If some go here and some go there,
do they divide up equally?

**How many grackles do
you see in the flock?**

How many grackles are in each group? What do you call two equal parts of a whole?

So ... nature knowing numbers?
No, not really true.
The only creatures to need numbers?
Actually, just you!

Nature Notes

 **Deciduous trees** like maples, oaks, and ashes lose their leaves every fall. The leaves turn red, orange, or yellow before falling to the ground. Many small creatures, such as the filmy dome spider, can survive the winter by burrowing in the fallen leaves.

 **Eastern gray squirrels** can be either gray or black in color. In the fall they store food for the winter. They save nuts such as acorns, walnuts, butternuts, hickory nuts, and pine seeds by burying them. They find them again in the winter by smell. Sometimes they don't find them all, and those buried nuts grow into new trees.

Milkweed pods dry and split open so the seeds, which are attached to fluffy parachutes, are blown by the wind to new places. Blackberry seeds are hidden inside the fruit. After an animal eats the berry, the seeds are left behind in its poop. The seeds might grow in that place.

Humpback whales migrate in groups to warmer tropical waters when the temperature starts to cool. They go there to give birth to their babies. The babies drink their mothers' milk, but the adults don't eat much in the tropical waters because they are unable to find their usual diet of small fish and krill. They live in the Pacific and Atlantic oceans.

Flocks of Canada geese fly south in the fall to warmer areas where the water and soil do not freeze. In the sky, they often fly in the shape of a V. The bird at the point of the V works hardest to move through the air, so the geese take turns flying in that position.

Pronghorn antelopes can run as fast as some cars — up to 86 km/hr. (53 mi./hr.). Every fall the herds migrate south to warmer areas where food and water are available. They live in grasslands or prairies. They don't drink much water because they get most of the water they need from the plants they eat.

Raccoons live both in the wild and in cities. They have five toes on all four paws. They sleep in the day and are active at night. In the wild they eat fruit and small creatures like crayfish, frogs, mice, crickets, and mollusks, but in the city they love to raid garbage cans.

Monarch butterflies migrate south in the fall. They fly by themselves during the day and at night gather in groups called roosts. There can be as many as thousands of monarchs at a nighttime roost. Roosts are usually in trees near a source of nectar.

Little **brown bats** gather together in the fall in underground caves or mines, where the temperature stays above freezing. Some bats will migrate to find these places. As many as ten thousand or more bats can be in one cave, called a hibernaculum. The bats hibernate hanging upside down.

Pikas live in mountain areas. They gather the grasses and wildflowers they like to eat and pile them in small haystacks. The plants dry in the sun, or the pikas move them about to help them dry. Then the pikas put the piles deep in their dens. They will eat this food in winter.

Black bears eat a lot of food in the late summer and fall because they need to build a layer of fat for the winter. They will eat almost anything, and they especially like berries, nuts, and roots. They look for a den, a place where they can curl up all winter, under tree stumps, in holes, or inside hollow trees.

Grackles that live in some parts of Canada and the northern United States migrate south in the fall. They are large, noisy birds that eat corn, seeds, small fish, leeches, acorns, grasshoppers, beetles, and caterpillars. They can form large flocks, often with other blackbirds and starlings. They roost in trees or on electrical power lines.

To Ryan, who counts in as 1 in 1,000,000 and always a 1st to me
~Lizann

To Meribeth, my mother and passionate teacher
~Ashley

The author wishes to acknowledge the support of the Ontario Arts Council through the Writer's Reserve program.

Owlkids Books Inc.
10 Lower Spadina Avenue, Suite 400, Toronto, Ontario M5V 2Z2
www.owlkids.com

Distributed in Canada by University of Toronto Press
5201 Dufferin Street, Toronto, Ontario M3H 5T8

Distributed in the United States by Publishers Group West
1700 Fourth Street, Berkeley, California 94710

Library and Archives Canada Cataloguing in Publication

Flatt, Lizann
    Counting on fall / written by Lizann Flatt ; illustrated by Ashley
Barron.

 (Math in nature)
Issued also in an electronic format.
ISBN 978-1-926973-36-4

    1. Mathematics--Juvenile literature. 2. Nature--Juvenile literature.
3. Autumn--Juvenile literature. I. Barron, Ashley II. Title.
III. Series: Flatt, Lizann. Math in nature.

 QA141.3.F63 2012   j513   C2011-908316-7

Library of Congress Control Number: 2011944603

Design: Claudia Dávila

Canadian Heritage / Patrimoine canadien

Canada

Ontario — Ontario Media Development Corporation — Société de développement de l'industrie des médias de l'Ontario

Canada Council for the Arts / Conseil des Arts du Canada

ONTARIO ARTS COUNCIL / CONSEIL DES ARTS DE L'ONTARIO

We acknowledge the financial support of the Canada Council for the Arts, the Ontario Arts Council, the Government of Canada through the Canada Book Fund (CBF) and the Government of Ontario through the Ontario Media Development Corporation's Book Initiative for our publishing activities.

Manufactured by C&C Joint Printing Co., (Guangdong) Ltd.
Manufactured in Shenzhen, China, in March 2012
Job No. HM1161

A   B   C   D   E   F

Owlkids — Publisher of Chirp, chickaDEE and OWL
www.owlkids.com